To Declan & Dominic   2022
All our love,
   Great-Grandma & Grandpa Bump

HAPPY, IS BEING THE BEST "YOU"
THAT "YOU" CAN BE.

Persistence and patience are the two words I live by when creating my unique, one-of-a-kind books. I want my books to stand-alone. I want you to look at the photos and say, "that can't be a real photograph." I take a lot of pride in saying, "yes...that is a real photograph! One click of the shutter, one moment in time." I want you to laugh, scratch your head, and wonder how I got wild animals to do what they're doing; not to mention, get the shot at the right moment.

To me, photography is meant to record history and the earth's natural beauty, not cut and paste several images into one and make it something that it's not. There is enough make believe in our world. I want to create something real, and I have. We all love a great fantasy story, but there is just something extra mystifying that grabs our attention and stays memorable in our heart when it's real.

This is extremely tedious, difficult, frustrating, time-consuming work because wild animals don't do what they're told. It's a process of earning their trust, then figuring out how to lead them to where I need them. Extreme calm and caution must be taken when being around wild animals. Although some may appear friendly, there is always a dangerous risk. Keep in mind, their entire focus is on survival and that's a mindset very few of us could ever fully understand.

Like the bear in this story, there are many cold or bug filled hot blistering days when I'm not real happy being myself. Those days when nothing goes right, the animals don't show up, or the lighting is horrible. Those are the days I constantly ask myself, "What am doing this for, and why?" Believe me, there are far more irritating days than there are satisfying moments. Most days are just a comedy show of bloopers and mishaps. Then, I get a shot like the cover of this book. A shot where it appears the bear sitting down is actually smiling as it's looking into the camera. In a split second, the comedy show of errors became the shot of a lifetime.

Once I finally beat the frustration and complete a project, the answers become clear. Take a look at the smile on yours and your children's faces as you turn through the pages of my books. As you laugh together and hear it echo through the room, that's when I know without question, I love what I do and I'm happy being me. I hope this book helps you find happiness being the special person that you are.
                                                           - Ron St. Germain

All Rights Reserved to Ron St. Germain. Original photographs, design and text are the protected property of Ron St. Germain. Unauthorized reproduction of any image, text, or design is punishable by law. This includes photocopying, scanning, photo postings on personal or non-personal web pages. Hard cover ISBN 978-0-9899721-3-0. First Printing - 1500 Copies, September 2018.
Published by - Bearwave Publications - Grand Ledge, Michigan. For questions and appearances contact Ron St. Germain at DaPhotoDude@aol.com - Facebook - www.Facebook.com/BearwaveBooks - Printed in Canada.

Because I'm A Bear

By Ron St. Germain

There once was a bear.
A sad, grumpy, grumbly bear.

"Good morning bear," said the little hare.
"How do you fare? Why the despair?"

"Why so gloomy and gray, gray, gray?" squawked the blue, blue jay.

"I don't like seeing you sad," said the raccoon. "Would you feel better if I sang you a tune?"

"So what's the prob, prob problem?"
chirped the red, red robin.

"Life just isn't fair, and it's because… I'm a bear."

"D   "Yes, it's true, we heard it too.
It didn't just come from out of the blue."

"Cute?" the porcupine asked with a shrug.
"Has anyone ever wanted a porcupine hug?"

"I should be a cardinal instead.
I'll dart through the trees a bright cherry red."

"But there's only one you, and only one me.
It's what's in your heart, not your color I see."

"Then I'll be a wolf. It would be fun I'd assume, to run with a pack and howl at the moon."

"Oh, but bear," the wolf said with a howl.
"Many would love to have your famous growl."

"I should be a photographer and take beautiful pictures to share."

"But most photographers," said the raccoon, "would rather take pictures of a bear."

"I'd like to be an opossum so I could pretend that I'm asleep."

"We only pretend when we get scared, while all winter, you fall asleep for weeks."

"I would love to hop, swim and croak.
Being a frog would be no joke."

"To be tiny like me might not be a prize.
Be glad that you're a thousand times my size."

"I think I'll be a chipmunk
and fill my cheeks with no room to spare."

"Funny," the chipmunk chipped,
"I was just pretending to be a bear."

"If I were a tortoise,
I could take my time where I go."

"Be glad you're fast," the tortoise laughed, "you may not like moving this slow."

"I'll be an owl," the bear said with a scowl.
"I'd have really big eyes and be oh so wise."

"Hooo," the owl hooted, " it's nice of you to say.
But, you can outsmart most, on any given day."

"I'll become a giraffe and stand so very tall."

"Well bear, if I tried to climb like you, I would surely fall."

"I'm being sincere, I want to be a deer, with antlers tall and strong."

"I'm very honored," the deer replied, "but my antlers don't last long."

"Stop right there," said Momma bear, "you should not dream to be something else."

"There is no shame in who you are.
Your greatest gift is to be yourself."

"Always remember; whenever you're torn, the world wasn't special until you were born."

The bear began to realize while taking a rest,
being a bear is special and truly it was blessed.

There wouldn't be Gummy bears or Teddy bears, and who could imagine that?

Little kids are just cuter catching snowflakes in bear hats.

Bears are used on signs to tell us fun and important stuff.

Many sports teams are named after bears, because bears are so tough.

With a paw on its chin,
the bear began to think for a while.

Suddenly, the thought of just being a bear brought on a big bear smile.

"When I look at my reflection...
I'm going to be proud of who I see."

"There is a lot about me to love,
so I shouldn't hide from being me."

"I shouldn't dream my life away to be something that I'm not."

"I should celebrate what I am and everything I've got."

"So, you wouldn't want to be a raccoon and wear a silly mask?"

"I think that mask looks best on you, but I'm really glad you asked."

"You wouldn't want to be a dolphin and swim with us in the open seas?"

"Thank you for the invitation, but I'd miss the forest and the trees."

"Why don't you wish to be a beaver and help me build a dam?"

"I can't keep wishing to be something I'm not, or I'd be wasting who I am."

"Jump in for a swim and be a beautiful swan."

"Thanks, but I'm looking pretty good just getting my bear on."

"I've learned a lot about myself and I know it's best for me,

to bury thoughts of what I'm not,
and be the best bear I can be."

"You don't want to be a chickadee, dee, dee?
You're no longer sad or in despair?"

"Nope, I'm just happy being me, me, me.
And, it's because... I'm a bear."

Big Bear Hug
Thank you to the Editors.
Tammy Morris Dohm
Patricia Anderson Leary

THE END...

The Bear Facts

Three species of bears in the United States

Polar Bear Grizzly Bear Black Bear

I win the race. The fastest human ran 28mph in a short sprint. Bears can run 25 to 35 mph for long distances.

A bear's preferred diet is herbs, fruit and grasses.

How Tall?
Black - 7ft.
Grizzly - 9ft.
Polar - 10ft.

A female bear is called a Sow. A male bear is called a Boar.

Baby bears are called cubs and stay with their mother up to two years. Only the female raises the cubs.

Bears can see color. Black bears can be various shades of black, white and brown.

Black and Grizzly bears hibernate for 5-7 months. Only pregnant Polar bears hiberante.

The oldest known bear was a grizzly who lived to be 56-years old. Average age of a wild bear is 18-25.

A polar bear can swim up to 100-miles without resting and smell up to 40-miles-away.

Bearwave Publications

Straight To Your Heart From America's Heartland

Like Us on Facebook

- Why Is Everyone Coming to My House? *By Ron St. Germain*
- Because I'm A Bear *By Ron St. Germain*
- MY MICHIGAN *By Ron St. Germain*
- I LOVE YOU MORE Than... *By Ron St. Germain*

Everybody LOVES a GREAT Story.

Reading A Bearwave Book will make you **Family Strong** And Laugh Out Loud

The first Teddy Bear went on sale February 15, 1903.

A collection worth having.

Nobody puts more into a book than I do. From the one-of-a-kind orignal photographs to the hidden things among the lovable pages, hours of fun and laughs await you and your family in each unique book. My books don't get old, they get worn out. Collect all of my books by visiting www.MKT.com/Bearwave-books. For multiple book orders contact DaPhotoDude@aol.com for savings on shipping rates, multiple book deals, wholesale opportunities and speaking events.
Love us on Facebook - www.Facebook.com/Bearwavebooks.